1

First published: June 2016

ISBN (Hard Cover): 9781943413027
ISBN (Soft Cover): 9781943413034

Visit us on the web!
www.tozknows.com

In addition to promoting literacy and biblical education to children, Toz Knows partners with non-profit and other charity organizations to give back to the community. For every TWO Toz Knows books purchased, ONE is donated to a child in need.

For more information regarding a partnership with Toz Knows, visit
www.tozknows.com/partners

Printed in the United States of America

Illustrator: Tina Modugno
www.tinamodugno.com

Toz Knows

THE THREE WHO DIDN'T BOW

Mindi Jo Furby & Kristin Lee Arnold

Illustrated by Tina Modugno

Tails wagging to and fro
Were Miley and little Toz.
They pranced about on their way home,
Saying, "Hurry, hurry, we must go!"

"Miley, oh Miley,
What can it be?
Is it news for you,
Or news for me?"

"Oh Toz, you silly boy.
Maybe it is just a toy!
All new and shiny
Large, not tiny!"

Possibilities they pondered;
Through the marshes they wandered.

"Hi Mom, hi Dad!
We are finally here!"
Toz and Miley were really glad
To see if a new toy was here.

"Miley and Toz, we have some news
And with it you must help us choose
The colors of the new nursery
For another sister you'll soon see!"

Love was on display
Sparking lots of barks,
Louder than the dog park!
Cheers! Hip hip hooray!

But In the midst,
Of kiss after kiss,
Stood Tozer quiet
In this happy riot...

7

On the next day
Toz exclaimed,
"Ole pal, ole buddy,
I'm feeling uneasy,
Even a little queasy,
Just really cruddy!

"Toz knows, Toz knows,
I'm going to have a new sis
And should be in bliss...
I'm super nervous though!"

As the White Bird flew by up high
In the blue Savannah sky,
Woody asked, "Why oh why?"

"That one boy at school
Is rotten and rude;
I'm sick of his 'tude,
He acts like a fool.
He makes kids do things
Like they're puppets on strings.

"How can I stand up
To this big bully
When he pressures me,
Our friends, or the new pup?"

"This reminds me, Toz,
Of the story with three guys
From way back in time,
You know how it goes?"

"Hmm, let me think,
Let me ponder,
Let my mind wander,
I'll know in a blink!"

They hemmed and hawed
And paced and pawed.
The White Bird then flew over
Sparking the mind of Tozer!

"Toz knows, Toz knows!
With a fire that's blazing,
A statue so amazing,
Three men oh so brave,
Stood up for God and gave
A mean king full of might
An unforgettable sight.
That's how the story goes!"

"That's the one, yippee!
Tell me the whole story,
The three men, God's glory!"
Woody barked happily.

The two pups laid down
On the cool Savannah ground.
Woody was ready to hear
Toz tell a story so dear.

"Long ago back in the day,
Were bad people who disobeyed.
The Israelites were frauds—
Serving idols, not the real God.

God told them all to share
His mighty truth with great care
To the nations all around
The young and old in every town.

But oh did they fail!
Yet God remained faithful
To them, loyal and stable
Even though they had bailed.

Because they were bad
And wouldn't say sorry,
God took a stand
In sadness and fury.

God sent a strong king
To conquer His people
Slaves now to be
No longer happy or peaceful.

Nebuchadnezzar was the king,
(Yes that's a mouthful!)
Who took over the Israelis
His army so powerful.

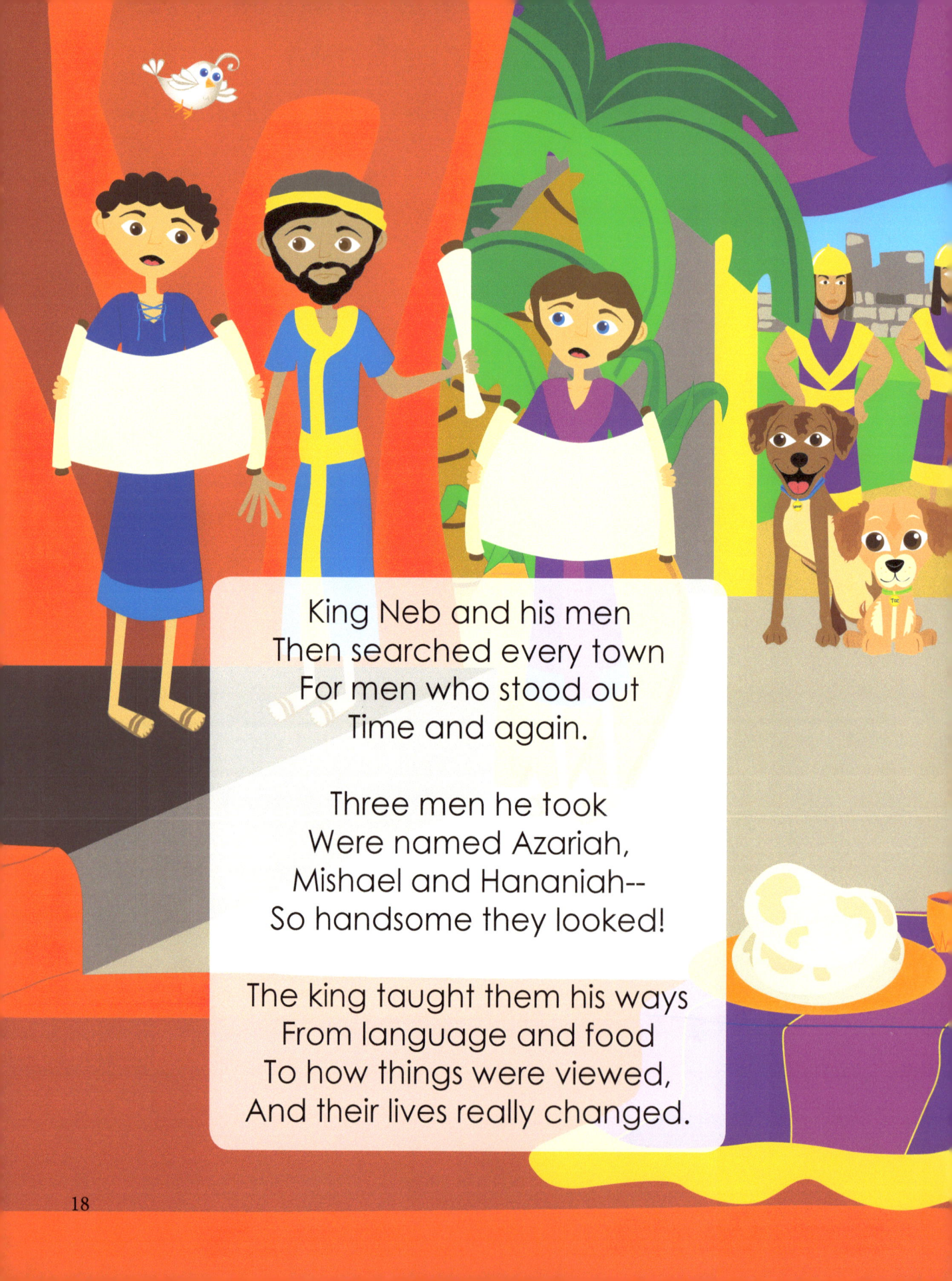

King Neb and his men
Then searched every town
For men who stood out
Time and again.

Three men he took
Were named Azariah,
Mishael and Hananiah--
So handsome they looked!

The king taught them his ways
From language and food
To how things were viewed,
And their lives really changed.

Babylonian they became-
Now called Meshach,
Abed-nego and Shadrach-
All funny new names.

Loyal they appeared
To all those near.
But true they remained
To the one and only God
Whom they loved above all,
Much to the king's disdain!

The king decided to create
A statue so large, so great.
Ninety feet and made of gold
In his image, it was bold.

When the music would sound
They were supposed to bow
Very low to the ground.
Standing would be daring
While the music was blaring.

If respect they didn't show
To the furnace they would go!
It was blazing hot
Survive it they would not.

Yet these were three men
Who would not bow down to him.

The king became upset
And issued them a threat.
But they still didn't bow
So they'd be punished now.

To the hot, raging fires
Of the furnace they went,
Their heads held high, not bent.
For they remained true
To the real God they knew,
Their courage was admired.

When Neb looked to the flames
He saw them standing, still the same.
Not a burn, but something new
Another Man had joined them too!

When he told them to come out
Surprised he was to see
Not a burn on the three
The king had much to think about!

If their God could protect them so
The most powerful He must be.
Everyone, even the king, could see.
This God everyone should know!

He declared a new rule
Because he'd been a fool,
The true God they would now serve
His laws they must now observe.

That night as Toz lay down
Sleep was nowhere to be found.
His mind kept playing the story
Of how the men brought God glory.
They stayed true and brave like Jesus did later;
They were all faithful to the end, never traitors.

Like the three men
Toz would stand and be brave.
The bully might then
Grow weary and cave.

The next day at school
Toz stood up to the bully.
With a prayer he stayed cool
Though his belly was jelly!

Everyone was shocked
By the courageous pup
Who bravely stood up
His beliefs firmly locked!

The bully backed down
Wearing a frown.
Toz then asked to be his friend,
And they made plans for the weekend!

As the months went by,
Mama June's belly grew.
It was then that Toz knew
His new sister would be fine
For she had a big brother,
A family, and a God so divine!

MEET THE TEAM!

Mindi Jo Furby
Co-Author / Publicist

Mindi Jo Furby is an author and speaker who dedicates her life to fighting biblical illiteracy one publication at a time. Equipped with a degree in Biblical Studies and a Masters in Religion, she loves helping others fall in love with God through the pages of His Word. She, her husband, daughter and pups make their home near Hilton Head, SC.

www.mindijofurby.com

Kristin Lee Arnold
Co-Author

Kristin Lee Arnold is a UNC Chapel Hill grad who's pursuing her Masters in Special Education at Armstrong University. She loves children and has an incredible talent for writing books that not only entertain, but teach them truths about life and God in new and exciting ways! She makes her home in Savannah, GA, along with her pup, Woody.

Kaci Ann Hollingsworth
Non-Profit Coordinator

Kaci Ann Hollingsworth is also a UNC Chapel Hill grad who loves non-profit organizations and initiatives. She currently works for a non-profit and volunteers with many others. She makes her home with her pup, Mackey, in Hilton Head Island, SC.

Tina Modugno
Children's Illustrator

Tina Modugno is an illustrator, author and publicist from Quebec, Canada. She has illustrated and published many titles including some of her own children's books. Tina is a huge animal advocate and lives with five feline family members. She is the creator of *"The Oreo Cat"* and through her work, she is dedicated to helping educate the public about the crippling side effects of feline declawing.

www.tinamodugno.com
www.theoreocat.com

www.ingramcontent.com/pod-product-compliance
Lightning Source LLC
LaVergne TN
LVHW072056070426
835508LV00002B/131